What Was
the Gold Rush?

by Joan Holub

illustrated by Tim Tomkinson

Grosset & Dunlap
An Imprint of Penguin Random House

For Elizabeth, Shelton, and Charlotte Ensley—JH

For Parker and Chase—TT

GROSSET & DUNLAP
Penguin Young Readers Group
An Imprint of Penguin Random House LLC

Text copyright © 2013 by Joan Holub.
Illustrations copyright © 2013 by Tim Tomkinson. All rights reserved.
Published by Grosset & Dunlap, an imprint of Penguin Random House LLC,
345 Hudson Street, New York, New York 10014. The WHO HQ™ colophon and
GROSSET & DUNLAP are trademarks of Penguin Random House LLC.
Printed in the USA.

Library of Congress Cataloging-in-Publication Data is available.

ISBN 978-0-448-46289-9   15 14 13 12 11

Contents

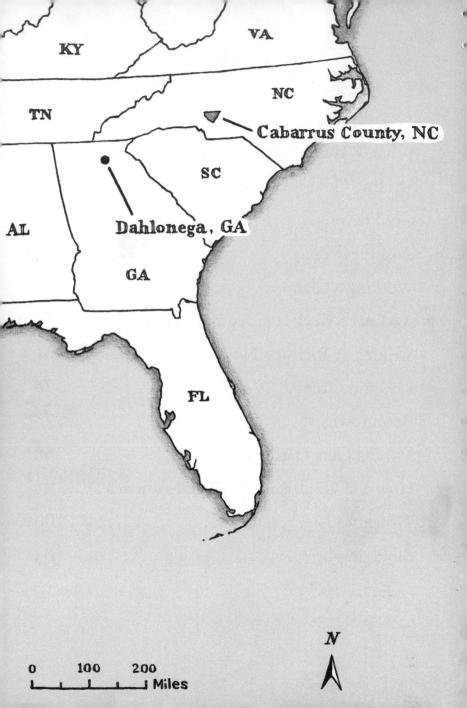

KY

VA

TN

NC

Cabarrus County, NC

SC

AL

Dahlonega, GA

GA

FL

0   100   200
|__|__|__|__| Miles

N

What Was the Gold Rush?

A gold rush happens when lots of people race off to where gold has just been discovered. They all expect to find gold and get rich. The first gold rush in the United States was in North Carolina in 1799. It began when a twelve-year-old boy found a seventeen-pound gold nugget in a creek. His family didn't know the nugget was gold, so they used it as a doorstop. Then, in 1802, they sold it for $3.50. They didn't know it was worth far more—over $350,000 in today's dollars! For fifty years, North Carolina produced more gold than any other state.

There was another gold rush in the Appalachian Mountains of Georgia thirty years later. The estimated amount of gold it produced every month in 1830 would be worth $14 million today.

But the most famous one is the gold rush of 1849. It happened when gold was discovered in California—gold worth billions of dollars today.

The biggest nugget found weighed 195 pounds—as much as a grown man weighs!

In 1849, the majority of people in the United States lived east of the Mississippi River. The states with the most people were New York, Pennsylvania, Ohio, and Virginia. After gold was discovered, people headed west hoping to get rich. The rumor was that gold was easy to find in California, but it might not last forever.

Men left their jobs and families in a hurry. These gold-hunters were called prospectors. They had other nicknames, such as "forty-niners." They were also called argonauts, after a group of treasure-seekers in a Greek myth.

It was a long trip. Most went overland by covered wagon or took ships from the East Coast that eventually wound up in California. Some walked, with only a wheelbarrow or bag to carry their stuff.

Hundreds of thousands of Americans and

A typical miner with his equipment

Pick

Water canteen

Pan

Bucket

Shovel

foreigners caught gold fever. People went half crazy over the idea of making a fortune. Some did get rich. Some got very, very rich. But most didn't.

Still, it was an exciting time. And it all started by accident!

CHAPTER 1
Striking Gold

The big day was January 24, 1848. The place was the American River in Coloma, California. This was in the foothills of the Sierra Nevada mountains.

A carpenter named James Marshall was building a sawmill there for John Sutter. The two

men were in business together. Sutter already had a fort, a cattle ranch, a farm, and a home nearby. When the sawmill was finished, it would cut trees into lumber. The lumber would be sold. Marshall and Sutter would each get an equal share of the profits from the lumber business.

The crew building the sawmill had dug a shallow canal. It branched off from the American River. Water from the river could flow into the canal. Electricity wouldn't be available until the late 1800s. The force of the running water would turn the mill's big wheel to operate the saw.

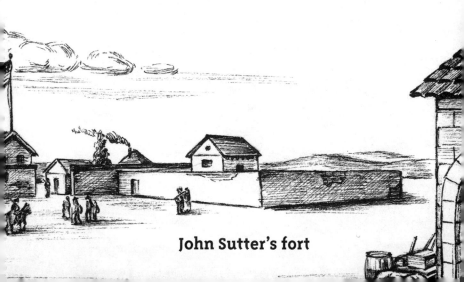

John Sutter's fort

Foothills of the Sierra Nevada in California—
where much of the gold was found.

James Marshall was checking the canal when he spotted something shiny. Looking closer, he saw small golden rocks and flakes. They were in the water behind the mill's wheel.

Quickly, he scooped some up in his hat. He went to show the men in his crew. *Is it gold?* they all wondered. Maybe it was only fool's gold. That was the nickname for a mineral called pyrite. It

looked like gold and often fooled miners. But pyrite was worthless.

Marshall knew that pyrite was brittle. Gold, however, was fairly soft and difficult to break. Taking a hammer, he pounded a few of the shiny pea-size nuggets. They didn't break. He boiled them in a pot of water with lye soap. He soaked the nuggets in vinegar. They didn't crumble or melt. It looked like he'd found gold!

Marshall must have been an honest man. He didn't try to hunt for more gold or keep it for himself. Instead, he rushed to Sutter with the nuggets.

Sutter was excited, too. But he still wasn't sure the nuggets were gold. So the two men checked an encyclopedia. It said that a gold nugget is about eight times heavier than a rock of the same size. They weighed a nugget against other kinds of rocks. It was much heavier. They dripped a liquid called nitric acid on it. Metals such as silver, copper, or pyrite would have melted. However, their nugget didn't.

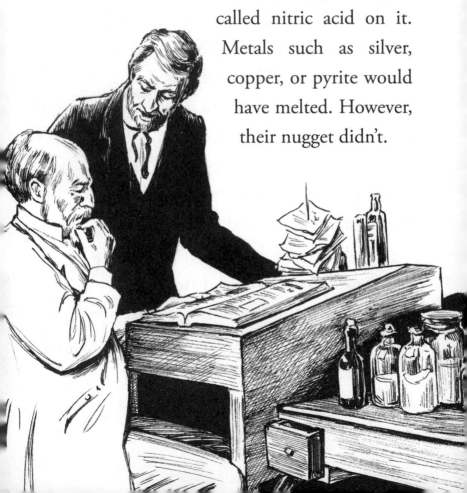

It was gold all right! They were going to be rich. Or so the two men thought.

Almost immediately, John Sutter began to worry. He didn't actually own the land where the gold had been found. He needed to gain control of it, and fast.

The United States had just defeated Mexico in the Mexican-American War. Soon the United States would own California. Then, any US citizen could claim 160 acres of public land in California for $1.25 an acre. But nobody could do that until Mexico signed a treaty.

A tribe of Nisenan Native Americans had lived on the land for more than a thousand years. Sutter

decided to work a couple of deals with them to take over the land. They weren't fair deals, though.

First, he signed a treaty with them. Next, Sutter tried to rent the land in exchange for shirts, handkerchiefs, knives, meat, flour, and peas. The land was worth a lot more than that.

Sutter's deals weren't legal, either. Only the US government had the power to make treaties. The government also claimed that Native Americans had no right to own land—even land they'd lived on long before white settlers arrived. And if they didn't own the land, they couldn't sell or rent it.

This was bad news for Sutter. If he had no legal claim on the land, anyone could dig for gold by the sawmill. He couldn't stop them.

How could he make sure no one else found out about the gold? By keeping it a secret. He asked Marshall and his crew not to tell anyone. But news this big would be hard to keep quiet for very long.

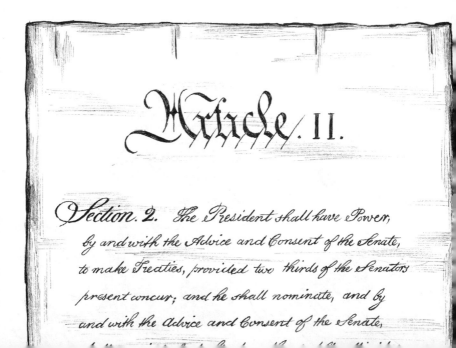

Article. II.

Section. 2. The President shall have Power, by and with the Advice and Consent of the Senate, to make Treaties, provided two thirds of the Senators present concur; and he shall nominate, and by and with the Advice and Consent of the Senate,

CHAPTER 2
Gold Fever

Work on the sawmill stopped immediately. Marshall's crew had seen the gold nugget. They figured there was more where that came from. So they began hunting for it. Sutter's farmhands soon heard about the gold, too. They left the farm and headed to the river to prospect. They knew they could make a lot more money by finding gold than by working the land.

At first, only those men who lived nearby came. They were checking out the rumors of gold. When they saw it for themselves, they told others.

Seven weeks after the first nuggets were found, a San Francisco newspaper ran a story. It wasn't a big story. The headline was simple: "Gold Mine Found." Only about eight hundred people lived in San Francisco back then. People who read the small article were curious. But they weren't sure whether to believe it.

In the 1860s, the Pony Express would begin cross-country mail service. Telegraph lines would connect the East and West Coasts. But in 1848, news of the gold strike traveled slowly—mostly by word of mouth.

John Sutter's secret was so exciting, however,

that even he had trouble keeping quiet. In February, he mentioned the gold in a letter to a friend. "I have made a discovery of a gold mine, which, according to experiments we have made, is extraordinarily rich."

That spring, one of Sutter's workers bought supplies at a store near the sawmill. He paid for them with gold he'd prospected. The owner of the supply store, Sam Brannan, lived in San

Francisco. When he heard about this, he headed to the sawmill. He didn't plan to become a miner himself. But he hoped to encourage others to go prospecting. Maybe he could get rich selling tools and supplies to them.

At Sutter's sawmill, Brannan found gold dust. Enough to fill a bottle. He took the bottle of gold dust back to San Francisco and showed it

off. He walked about the streets yelling, "Gold from the American River!" Many who heard him dropped everything to go prospecting on the land surrounding Sutter's sawmill.

By that summer, there were four thousand gold-hunters in the Sierra Nevada. In July, a ship going north from San Francisco to Oregon spread the news. In August, word reached the East Coast. A New York newspaper printed the headline

"GOLD! Gold from the American River!" By December, there were ten thousand prospectors in California.

US president James K. Polk was excited by the news from California, too. Like many Americans at that time, he believed in the idea of Manifest Destiny. That meant he thought US citizens had the right and the duty to spread out across America from the East Coast to the West Coast. Manifest Destiny was really just an excuse to seize land and resources. The president wanted more people to move west and settle there. And the chance to find gold was a good reason for people in the East to head west. On December 5, President Polk announced that the rumors of gold in California were true.

What Is Gold?

It's a bright golden-yellow metal. Most other metals are gray.

It's a chemical element. That means it's naturally pure—not mixed with anything else.

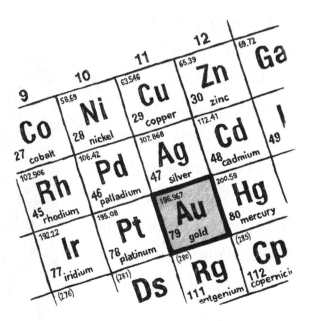

The standard measurement for gold is called troy weight. An ounce of gold is about the size of two jelly beans. One ounce can be hammered into a paper-thin sheet big enough to carpet a whole room.

President
James K. Polk

The president's word was as good as gold. People in the East caught gold fever.

The California gold rush was on!

John Sutter had been right to worry. He ended up worse off than before the gold was found. He couldn't stop miners from coming. All of his workers at the farm, fort, and ranch went off prospecting. The fruit in his orchard was rotting on the trees. There was no one left to pick it.

Crops weren't planted or harvested. His cattle weren't cared for. So far, the gold rush had been nothing but trouble for him.

Why Is Gold Worth So Much?

First of all, gold is rarer than most other metals. And it usually costs a lot to mine gold.

Also, it doesn't corrode. That means it'll last practically forever. Gold coins lost in shipwrecks don't rust in salt water. In Egypt, King Tut's golden treasures are three thousand years old. But they still look new.

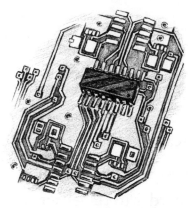

Gold is not magnetic. It conducts heat and electricity. So it's used to make parts inside TVs, computers, and other electronics. That also makes it valuable.

Over half of all gold is used to make jewelry. That's because it's shiny and beautiful, and it doesn't break easily. It's one of the most bendable, poundable metals.

Look for the tiny stamp on gold jewelry. Pure gold is stamped 24k—twenty-four karats. Gold that's mixed with another metal will have a lower number, usually 18k or 14k.

CHAPTER 3
Rushing West

By the time the news spread to the East Coast in 1848, it was almost winter again. Snow and cold weather made it much harder to travel across the country to California. So people—thousands of them—waited until the spring of 1849. By then, there would be grass growing on the plains to feed their animals on the trip west.

Soldiers deserted the army. Sailors left their ships. Teachers, lawyers, farmers, blacksmiths, and shopkeepers quit their jobs. Most were unmarried men. Those men who were married usually went alone. For one thing, they couldn't afford to bring their families. And they thought life in gold country would be too hard on women and children. Besides, most men didn't expect to stay in California for long. They expected to strike gold and return home rich.

There were three main ways to get to California from the eastern United States. Each way was hard and dangerous. In 1848 and 1849, about forty-one thousand people went by sea in 697 ships. About forty-eight thousand went overland.

Going overland was the cheapest way. To stay safe, travelers formed groups called wagon trains. Trails were rugged, so wagons pulled by oxen went slowly. If you walked, you could keep up with the wagons. But your shoes wore out fast, and your feet would get awfully sore.

Wagons crossed rivers, prairies, deserts, and steep mountains on the trip. West of Ohio, the country was mostly unsettled. There were no people or houses for many miles around.

It took seven months to get to California from East Coast cities such as New York. Two other major starting points were the Missouri cities of St. Joseph and Independence. From the Midwest, the trip was two thousand miles long and took five months. The Oregon, California, and Santa Fe Trails were the most popular wagon routes to the West.

Most overland travelers made it to California if they stayed on schedule. They had to leave Missouri by the end of April in order to make it through the Sierra Nevada mountains before winter came. Otherwise, they might get trapped in the snow.

Many "overlanders" faced plenty of problems. Like accidents and snakebites. Or running out of food and water. Or broken wagons and injured oxen. Cholera was caused by drinking water polluted by bacteria. It killed 1,500 travelers in 1849.

Prospectors who could afford it went to California by sea. They paid fares of $200 to $1,000. Going by ship was faster than traveling by wagon train.

There were two main sea routes from the East Coast. Both usually sailed southward on the Atlantic Ocean from New York or Boston.

The longer route went around Cape Horn. That's at the southern tip of South America. From there, ships sailed north on the Pacific Ocean to San Francisco. This route was almost 15,000 miles long. It usually took five or six months to

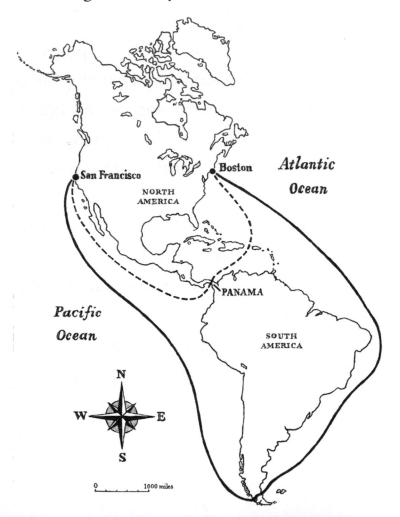

complete the journey. Fast clipper ships like the *Flying Cloud* could make the trip in three months. But there weren't enough of them to take everyone who wanted to go.

The shorter sea route (only 5,300 miles) went down the Atlantic coastline only as far as the Isthmus of Panama. The isthmus was a fifty-mile-wide strip of land connecting North America and South America. The east coast of Panama is on the Atlantic Ocean. Its west coast is on the Pacific.

The Panama Canal

In 1855, a railroad was built across the Isthmus of Panama. Then, in 1880, France began digging a canal across the isthmus. The French eventually ran out of money and stopped. In 1904, the United States, under President Theodore Roosevelt, took over the project. It took ten more years to complete the canal.

There were many problems during construction, such as landslides, heavy rains, thick jungles, accidents, and disease. More than twenty-seven thousand workers died in thirty-four years of building the canal.

The finished canal was fifty-two miles long. It still connects the Atlantic and Pacific Oceans today. The *SS Ancon* was the first ship to pass through the canal in 1914. Today, about forty ships take the three-hour trip through the canal every day. Panama is widening the canal so that bigger ships can use it starting in 2014.

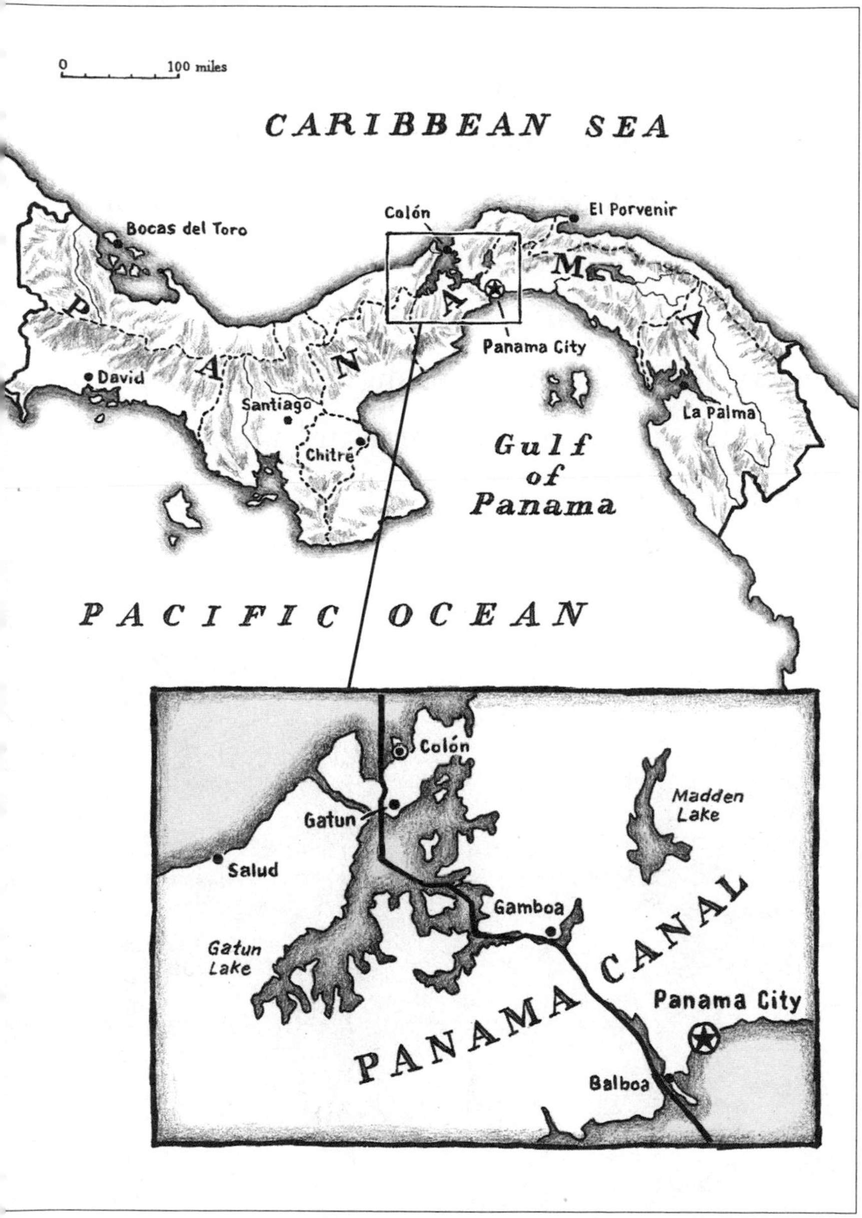

CARIBBEAN SEA

0   100 miles

Bocas del Toro

Colón

El Porvenir

P A N A M A

Panama City

David

Santiago

Chitré

Gulf
of
Panama

La Palma

PACIFIC OCEAN

Colón

Madden
Lake

Gatun

Salud

Gamboa

Gatun
Lake

PANAMA CANAL

Panama City

Balboa

At the isthmus, passengers got off their ships. They went forty miles up Panama's Chagres River in wooden canoes. Then, they traveled on mules through a jungle to Panama City on the Pacific side. There were wild animals such as alligators and monkeys in the jungle. Panama is near the equator. It was hot and humid. Some travelers caught diseases such as malaria and yellow fever from mosquitoes.

If all went well, the trip across the isthmus took only six weeks. However, prospectors might have to wait weeks in Panama City before a ship would arrive that was bound for San Francisco.

Today, traveling by ship often means enjoying a floating vacation. But life aboard a ship in the 1840s and 1850s was very different. The food had bugs and mold. The drinking water wasn't always clean. Sometimes ships ran out of both before the trip was over. There were rats on board. If passengers were injured or sick, they were on their own. There might not be a doctor to help them. There were terrible storms, especially near Cape Horn. Some ships sank.

Still, ships left for California almost every day in 1849. Shipping companies advertised all around the world for passengers. This fueled gold fever in faraway places such as China, Australia, and Europe. But the ads didn't mention the problems passengers would face on the voyage.

Many prospectors kept diaries and sent letters home. A man named S. Shufelt, who sailed from New York to California in 1849, wrote in a letter to his cousin, "I have left those that I love as my own life behind & risked every thing and endured many hardships to get here, & I want to make enough to live easier & do some good with, before I return."

Like all forty-niners, he hoped his struggles would pay off. In gold!

CHAPTER 4
Working a Claim

Once ships docked in San Francisco, the journey wasn't over. It was another 140 miles inland to the goldfields. Prospectors had to buy a tent, tools, and supplies.

Everything was more expensive in San Francisco than back east. But prospectors paid the high prices. They figured they'd soon strike it rich. If men were too poor to buy supplies, rich businessmen might grubstake them. That meant they'd lend them tools or money.

In return, the businessmen would share the gold that the prospectors found.

Most prospectors had never lived in a tent. They'd never hunted for gold before. They knew nothing about mining. They were easy to trick. Dishonest merchants sold them fake gold-finding gadgets. Or a skin cream that supposedly attracted gold flakes like a magnet. Prospectors could buy books about where to find gold. However, the maps and the mining instructions in them were often wrong.

San Francisco circa 1850

As soon as they could, prospectors dashed off to the goldfields. They usually settled in mining camps. There were many along the rivers. They had names like Bedbug, Hangtown, and Murderer's Gulch.

A sharp bend in a stream was a good place to look for gold. So was a deep riverbed. Any place gold might get caught and sink. When he found

a good spot, a prospector would claim it. If he wanted land along a river, he wasn't allowed to claim much. Maybe only ten square feet. Those were the rules. That way, no one could hog a good location.

To mark his area, a miner hammered stakes at its four corners. Or he might pile rocks. This was called staking a claim. He'd leave his mining tools on the claim to keep dibs on it. And he couldn't stay away for long. After a week, a claim was up for grabs. Anyone could take it. Of course, it was easy to stake a claim. The real work was getting the gold out.

In 1848, gold could be found lying here and there in California streams. How did it get there? Long ago, it had formed deep inside the earth. It melted and flowed into gaps between rocks such as granite or quartz. These gold-filled gaps are called veins or lodes.

When the rocks shifted over time, bits of gold

cracked loose. Heavy rains washed them out into rivers and streams. This loose gold is called placer gold. Sometimes it's easy to spot. Sometimes it's hidden under a few inches of gravel in a streambed.

The simplest way to find placer gold was by panning. A miner scooped gravel and water from a streambed into his pan. Then he swirled the pan around. Gold is heavier than water, dirt, sand, or gravel. So it sank to the bottom of the pan.

Next, the miner tilted the pan and swirled out the water and gravel. He did this many times until only gold was left in his pan. If there *was* any gold, that is. Most scoops brought up just gravel. If there *was* gold, miners called it "hitting pay dirt."

Panning was slow work. Things went faster with several men working a rocker or sluice. Those machines did the same job that a pan did.

Prospecting for gold was hard work. A man wound up squatting, kneeling, or standing all day. He carried buckets full of dirt or water. He shoveled gravel. He moved rocks. He waded waist-deep into cold rivers. His back hurt. His knees hurt.

And after all his hard work, there might not be a single speck of gold for a reward. It was easy to get discouraged.

A Miner's Tools

A knife to loosen nuggets. A pick to break up rock. A shovel to move dirt, rock, sand, and gravel.

A round tin pan with a flat bottom and raised sides was best for gold panning. It might also get used as a cooking pan. After cooking, any oil had to be washed away. Oil is gooey, and it floats. Gold flakes could stick to it and float to the top of the pan. They might spill out with the water and gravel and be lost!

A rocker was a wooden box about three feet long. The box sat atop rockers like those on a rocking chair. One prospector shoveled gravel from a streambed. He dumped it onto a grate or board full of holes set across the top end.

A second prospector poured water over that. A third rocked the box. Water, gold, and gravel washed through the grate. Then they tumbled over a series of small boards along the bottom of the box. Gravel and water whooshed out the bottom of the box. Any gold was caught by the small boards and stayed in the rocker.

A sluice was a long, narrow wooden chute. It could separate gold from bigger loads of dirt and rock. A sluice called a Long Tom might be up to fourteen feet long. It could only be used in areas with fast-running water.

CHAPTER 5
A Miner's Week

Today, most people work eight hours a day, five days a week. But a miner worked twelve to sixteen hours a day. And after his prospecting was done, he still had to cook dinner. Many men had never cooked a meal before. Dinner might be only beans, bacon, and coffee. Fruit and vegetables were scarce. Without them, a prospector could get a disease called scurvy. It came from not getting enough vitamin C.

Hardly anyone took a bath. Beards grew long. No one wanted to waste time washing clothes. They figured all that could wait till after they struck it rich.

Miners sometimes banded together in small groups. That way they didn't get so lonely. They

could share a tent. They could share expenses and work, too. If one miner got sick or was injured, his partners could take care of him.

Camp doctors weren't trustworthy. Sometimes they were only swindlers pretending to be doctors. They'd give a spoonful of flavored sugar water to a patient and say it was medicine. Then they'd charge up to a hundred dollars!

Miners at work in the goldfields

Some wives did come west to help out their husbands. But there were hardly ever any kids in the camps. The few who were there didn't go to school. They might help out at the mines. Or they got town jobs to earn money for the family. They delivered newspapers, swept shop floors, and ran errands in hotels.

Wives gardened, did laundry, and sometimes even mined. They also did the cooking. In September 1849, a prospector saw a woman named Luzena Wilson cooking outside her family's tent. He longed for home-cooked food. So he paid her ten dollars for a biscuit! That's the same as $250 today.

At night, sometimes miners gathered together to drink alcohol or gamble. They'd play simple games like outdoor bowling. They'd sing songs like "Oh! Susanna."

Sometimes bands of musicians or troops of actors came by the camps. This was a special treat. A little girl named Lotta Crabtree toured mining camps with her mother. She sang and danced for the miners. Everywhere she went, audiences tossed gold coins at her feet. When she was older, she performed in San Francisco and New York. By the time she died, she was worth $4 million.

Sometimes miners made trips to Stockton or Sacramento. Or even all the way to San Francisco. Miners had their gold nuggets and gold dust weighed at banks. They were paid by the weight of their gold. A pinch of gold dust was worth about a dollar.

In town, men bought more supplies. They'd also drink, dance, and gamble. Sometimes all night long. Only three out of every hundred people in California were women. Since there were hardly any women around, men danced with each other.

They grew tired of only seeing other rough, dirty men all the time, though.

Prospectors liked to get their photos taken in town. They'd pose with their mining tools and gold nuggets. If they didn't have any, the photographer might lend some gold for the picture. Miners would send these photos home to

show off a little. Or to comfort their families who missed them.

Sunday was a day off. Everyone did chores, wrote letters home, or hunted animals for food. Some held prayer meetings. Or they rested up for another long, hard week ahead.

Most miners were tired, worried, lonely, homesick, dirty, smelly, and broke. What kept them going? The thought that, any day now, they'd find gold. Other people had! All they needed was a little luck.

CHAPTER 6
Striking It Rich (or Not)

In 1849, a lucky miner might earn $2000 of gold a day from prospecting. But an average miner only earned between $5 and $30 a day. And everything was expensive in gold country. Boots could cost $20 and wore out fast. Two eggs might cost $1. A barrel of flour sometimes sold for $40. The average miner's $30 of gold didn't stretch very far.

Luck played a big part in who got rich and who didn't. On two claims right next to each other, one miner might find gold and the other nothing. You just never knew.

John Sutter turned out to be one of the most unlucky people. Within months after the gold strike, his ranch was falling apart. Prospectors stole his cattle and trampled his farm. Feeling desperate, he decided to go prospecting. He hired a crew to help him search for gold. No luck. He lost even more money.

Sutter's bookkeeper, however, was far luckier. His name was John Bidwell. In July 1848, he discovered gold along the Feather River, about ninety miles north of Sutter's sawmill. By the end of 1849, he'd found gold worth about $2.5 million in today's dollars. The location of his strike quickly grew into a mining camp of six hundred people. It was called Bidwell's Bar.

There were other famous finds. Some miners

became millionaires almost overnight. Two brothers named John and Daniel Murphy came to California in 1844 and began prospecting in the Sierra Nevada mountains in 1848. In less than two years, they made about $2 million in gold!

An army officer named John Frémont struck it rich, too. First, he tried to buy some land near San Francisco. By mistake, he bought land in the Sierra Nevada foothills instead. Frémont was angry about this. Still, he hired a crew of Mexican miners to look for gold on his new land. Soon, three sacks arrived at his doorstep. They held a hundred pounds of gold! And there was plenty more to come.

Stories like these encouraged other miners to keep trying. Everyone hoped to find the "mother lode," the main source of all California gold. No one ever found it, because it didn't exist. Instead, there were many gold deposits throughout the Sierra Nevada.

Sam Brannan moved to California in 1846 with a group of Mormon settlers. He started the *California Star*, which was the first newspaper in San Francisco.

In 1848, he spread the word about the gold strike at Sutter's sawmill. Then, he bought nearly all the iron pans in San Francisco for 20¢ each. He resold them to prospectors to use for gold panning, for $8 to $16 each. During 1849, his store at Sutter's fort made $150,000 a month. He opened more supply stores in nearby towns and bought land in California and Hawaii. He became one of California's first millionaires and one of its first state senators.

Miners were always looking for a home-cooked meal. One woman said she made $18,000 selling meat pies to hungry miners. That was a fortune in the 1850s.

Other women made as much as $100 a week doing laundry. Back east, women couldn't get well-paying jobs. But in gold country, the rules were different. Any hard worker with a good idea could earn a decent living. Even if they didn't go prospecting.

Some fabulous tales of riches sounded too good to be true. Still, the stories got passed around. One was about a lake of gold. A man named Thomas Stoddard claimed to have found the lake when he got lost near the Sierra Valley and Downieville. He said there were chunks of gold lying on its shores. His story spread quickly. Soon, more than five hundred miners paid him a fee to guide them to the lake. He tried, but he never could find it again. The men who'd paid him felt tricked. But he sneaked out of camp before they could get back at him.

Not everyone who came to California tried to hunt gold. Instead, they found other ways to make money from the gold rush. They started new businesses. They figured out what miners needed. And then they sold it to them. One thing miners needed was sturdy work clothes. A man named Levi Strauss opened a store in San Francisco. Levi's jeans are still sold today.

Levi Strauss

Levi Strauss was born in Bavaria, Germany, and moved to San Francisco in 1850. He had a business selling things such as umbrellas, handkerchiefs, underwear, and fabric to small stores throughout the West. These stores then sold the items to miners and settlers.

In 1873, he went into business with one of his customers—a tailor named Jacob Davis from Nevada.

They made blue denim pants with metal rivets on the pockets and seams. This added strength so the pants wouldn't rip.

Denim fabric was made in Nîmes, France. The word "denim" comes from "de Nîmes," which means "of Nîmes." A similar fabric came from Genoa, Italy. The French word for "Genoa" is "Genes." The two fabrics got confused, and the pants became known as jeans.

But in the 1800s, miners called the pants "waist overalls." They loved the pants because they lasted. Strauss sold them as fast as he could make them.

CHAPTER 7
Law and Order

California was a lawless place during the gold rush years. The earlier gold strikes in Georgia and North Carolina had been more orderly. They both were already states when gold was found, with laws, courts, and police to control crime. California didn't become a state until about two and a half years after gold was discovered at Sutter's sawmill.

Before statehood, mining camps came up with basic rules to keep things fair. A man named James Hutchings published a list of rules in a newspaper. It was called "The Miners' Ten Commandments." The list included good advice like: Don't stake more than one claim at a time, don't steal another's claim, and don't gamble away your gold.

In the early days of the gold rush, there wasn't much crime. Most people followed an honor system. A miner could safely leave his gold in his tent. It probably wouldn't get stolen.

But as more people came, the camps got crowded. Things changed. It wasn't as easy to find gold. There was more competition. Some miners got worried and greedy. Their families back home were counting on them to strike it rich. So they stopped following the rules. If they got really desperate, they might cheat, steal, or kill for gold. When a fellow miner wasn't around, they'd prospect his claim. This was called claim jumping. It was one of the most serious crimes.

Not all trouble in the camps was caused by miners. Criminals also came west. In California, no one knew about their pasts. They'd start

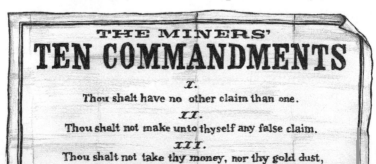

THE MINERS'

TEN COMMANDMENTS

I.

Thou shalt have no other claim than one.

II.

Thou shalt not make unto thyself any false claim.

III.

Thou shalt not take thy money, nor thy gold dust,

committing crimes all over again. The camps got more and more dangerous. At first, most claims had been along the rivers. When those were taken, prospectors moved into the mountains. Now they were far away from the busy camps. There was no one to help if a miner was robbed or attacked.

Prospectors took the law into their own hands. They decided among themselves whether someone was guilty of a crime. There was usually no trial. If there was, it was quick and unfair. Rule-breakers were treated harshly. The softest punishment was banishment from the camp. Worse punishments included whipping, branding, or cutting off an ear. Worst of all was death by hanging. There were many hangings in Hangtown. That is how the camp got its name.

As time went on, the miners who hadn't found much gold got angry and frustrated. They blamed miners who came from other countries. They thought it wasn't fair for foreigners to be

allowed to prospect in the United States. Only US citizens should be allowed to hunt for gold, they said. Their protests resulted in the Foreign Miners Tax in 1850. Miners who came from outside the United States now had to pay a lot of money for licenses.

In 1848, there were three people from China in California. By 1852, there were about twenty thousand. They called California *Gum Shan*, which meant "gold mountain." Chinese miners worked hard. They were good at their jobs. But they were treated unfairly.

In some places, Chinese were only allowed to mine abandoned claims. These were worthless mines others had given up on. Even so, Chinese workers still often managed to find gold in them.

Native American tribes were angry at miners. Who could blame them? The Nisenan, Maidu, Miwok, Yokuts, and Pomo tribes had lived in California's gold country for a thousand years before gold brought a rush of people west. The tribes didn't like how they and their land were being treated. For instance, newcomers shot buffalo for their hides or just for fun.

Prospectors didn't take good care of the land. They did whatever they had to do to reach gold. Sometimes they built dams. This dried up some rivers. Their digging muddied the streams. The sun could no longer reach plants and animals that lived in the water. Fish died. Water became polluted. Natural habitats were being wrecked.

Native Americans depended on the land for food and water. Now many went hungry. They raided miners' supply wagons to keep from starving. Angry miners burned their villages, sometimes killing them. But even more Native

Americans died from the new diseases miners had brought west, such as smallpox, cholera, dysentery, and measles.

Although California became a state on September 9, 1850, law and order came slowly. Bandits, criminal gangs, and murderers would roam its mining camps, hills, and towns for years to come.

Miners posing with their tools: rockers, wheelbarrows, picks, shovels, pans

James Marshall

John Sutter

Group of miners

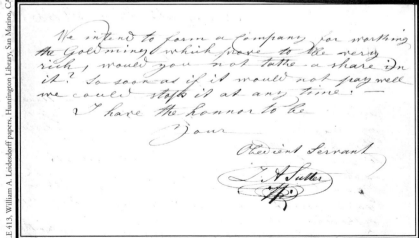

We intend to form a Company for working the Gold mines which prove to be very rich, would you not take a share in it? So soon as if it would not pay well we could stop it at any time! —

I have the honnor to be

Your

Obedient Servant

J A Sutter

John Sutter's letter sharing news of the Gold Rush

Bar Room in the Mines

Long Tom.

Lith & Published by Britton & Rey S. F.

Miners relaxing at a saloon (top); miners at work (bottom)

SUNDAY MORNING

Scenes of what miners might have done on Sundays

A PASSAGE TO THE GOLD REGION FOR $75 !

FOR SAN FRANCISCO DIRECT.

THE SPLENDID A. No. 1 NEWLY COPPERED

PACKET SHIP APOLLO.

recently in the European trade, having most of her freight engaged, will sail for

SAN FRANCISCO, CALIFORNIA,

and the gold region in that vicinity, from the

Foot of Chambers Street, North River,

WHERE SHE NOW LIES, ON THE SECOND OF JANUARY NEXT.

Passengers will be taken on the following terms ;

Steerage Passage - - - - - -	**$ 75.**
Cabin Passage - - - - - - - -	**150.**
Ditto out and home - - - - - -	**200·**
Ditto with board while there	**250.**

Several Families can be Accommodated.

The advantages offered to passengers by this conveyance cannot be surpassed. The APOLLO is one of the safest and most airy ships in New York, and has few equals in speed. She is destined to sail *directly*, not only for San Francisco, but, if it can be done as is expected, she is to be taken up the Sacramento river thirty or forty miles, into the very heart of the Gold Region, where she is to remain for some time.

The voyage each way, it is expected will be made in about four months.

Persons intending to take passage by this vessel will do well to secure their berths *at the earliest possible moment*, as the ship will, in a day or two be occupied entirely by Carpenters, Stevedores and other Mechanics, busily engaged in fitting up berths, stowing freight, taking in a supply of provisions, and making other preparations for the voyage. Choice of Berths will be given to passengers in the order of the numbers upon their passage tickets.

Freight taken on consignment or otherwise, at the lowest rates.

No Passage secured until paid for.

An 1849 advertisement listing prices

for passage to San Francisco

Miner posing
with pick

Price 25 Cents.

INSTRUCTIONS

FOR COLLECTING, TESTING, MELTING AND ASSAYING

GOLD.

WITH A DESCRIPTION OF THE PROCESS FOR DISTINGUISHING
NATIVE GOLD FROM THE WORTHLESS ORES WHICH ARE
FOUND IN THE SAME LOCALITY, AND THE CHEMICAL
TESTS AND NECESSARY APPARATUS TO BE
USED FOR TESTING GOLD, SILVER,
PLATINA AND MERCURY;

ILLUSTRATED WITH 30 WOOD ENGRAVINGS,

AND ARRANGED FOR THE USE OF PERSONS WHO ARE
ABOUT TO VISIT

THE GOLD REGION OF CALIFORNIA.

By EDWARD N. KENT, PRACTICAL CHEMIST,
No 116 JOHN-STREET, NEW-YORK.

☞ The whole of the Apparatus described in this work may be obtained as
above, at the prices mentioned in the Catalogue at the end.

Published by the Author.

NEW-YORK:
EDWARD N. KENT, PRACTICAL CHEMIST,
No. 116 JOHN STREET.
1849.

One of the first how-to
books for miners

CALIFORNIA
AND THE
GOLD REGION DIRECT!

The Magnificent, Fast Sailing and favorite packet Ship,

JOSEPHINE,
BURTHEN 400 TONS, CAPT.

Built in the most *superb* manner of Live Oak, White Oak and Locust, for a New York and Liverpool Packet; thoroughly Copper-fastened and Coppered. She is a very fast sailer, having crossed the Atlantic from Liverpool to New-York in 14 days, the shortest passage ever made by a *Sailing Ship*. Has superior accommodations for Passengers, can take Gentlemen with their Ladies and families. Will probably reach ☞ SAN FRANCISCO **THIRTY DAYS** ahead of any Ship sailing at the same time. Will sail about the

10th November Next.

For Freight or Passage apply to the subscriber,

RODNEY FRENCH,

New Bedford, October 15th. **No. 103 North Water Street, Rodman's Wharf.**

An advertisement for passage to California

1849

THE CALIFORNIA GOLD DIGGERS

Song and Chorus

As sung by the

Hutchinsons and Barkers

with rapturous applause

THE WORDS BY

JESSE HUTCHINSON JR

Music adapted and arranged

BY

Nathan Barker.

SPRINGFIELD S.W. MARSH *Main St.*

PHILADELPHIA,
E.L. WALKER *160 Chesnut St.*

Entered according to Act of Congress in the year 1849 by S.W. Marsh & Co. in the Clerks Office of the District Court of Mass.

Sheet music cover
for a song about
the miners

A NEW

DESCRIPTION OF OREGON

AND

CALIFORNIA:

CONTAINING

Complete Descriptions of those Countries,

TOGETHER WITH THE

OREGON TREATY AND CORRESPONDENCE,

AND A VAST AMOUNT OF INFORMATION RELATING TO THE

SOIL, CLIMATE, PRODUCTIONS, RIVERS AND S,

AND THE VARIOUS ROUTES OVER

THE ROCKY MOUNTAINS,

BY L. W. HASTINGS, A RESIDENT OF CALIFORNIA.

ALSO AN ACCOUNT, BY COL. R. B. MASON, OF THE

GOLD REGION,

AND A NEW ROUTE TO CALIFORNIA.

CINCINNATI: GEO. CONCLIN.
1849

Title page of an 1849
travel guide to Oregon
and California

One of the earliest photographs to show Chinese miners

James Marshall at Sutter's sawmill

Hoisting wheel, used to remove material from a mine

A rare photograph of a woman during the Gold Rush

An African American miner

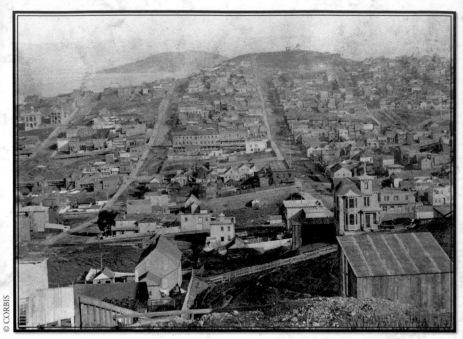

Home to immigrants, Telegraph Hill, San Francisco, during the Gold Rush

Coin featuring
a forty-niner

Gold nugget believed to be
the first piece of gold found
at Sutter's sawmill

The Miners' Ten Commandments

An 1850 photograph of the San Francisco harbor

CALIFORNIAN

BY B. R. BUCKELEW.

SAN FRANCISCO, MARCH 15, 1848.

GOLD MINE FOUND.—In the newly made raceway of the Saw Mill recently erected by Captain Sutter, on the American Fork, gold has been found in considerable quantities. One person brought thirty dollars worth to New Helvetia, gathered there in a short time. California, no doubt, is rich in mineral wealth; great chances here for scientific capitalists. Gold has been found in almost every part of the country.

San Francisco newspaper announcing gold found

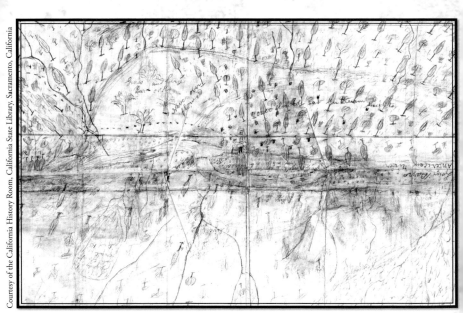

James Marshall's sketch mapping the gold discovery site

Native American Reservations

In the 1830s, the US government forced tribes of Native Americans in the East—such as the Choctaw, Chickasaw, Seminole, Creek, and Cherokee—to move west of the Mississippi River. Thousands of Native Americans died on the long trip west to the Great Plains. Twenty years later, the California gold rush brought many new prospectors and settlers west of the Mississippi River. They took over the land where Native Americans from the East had been sent. They also moved onto land where Native Americans in the West had lived for centuries. In 1851, the US government decided to create areas of land called reservations. They made Native Americans move from their homelands onto these reservations. Today, there are about three hundred such reservations in the United States.

CHAPTER 8
Boomtowns

Besides being dangerous, prospecting was also boring. Miners were eager to escape work and have some fun.

Throughout the Sierra Nevada foothills, many small towns seemed to spring up overnight. The population exploded. So gold rush towns were nicknamed boomtowns. Boomtowns were rowdy, busy places. They had small restaurants, saloons, dance halls, and general stores. Sometimes a merchant simply laid a board across two barrels on the street. Then he set his wares out to sell to passersby.

Sacramento and Stockton were the closest towns to Sutter's sawmill. Both grew with lightning speed during the gold rush. In April

1849, the population of Sacramento was 150 people. Six months later, 6,000 people lived there. Almost all of them were men.

Hotels and theaters were built. Musicians, opera singers, and actors came to perform. If they liked a show, miners might toss coins or gold onto the stage. If they didn't, they might throw rotten food or trash!

The most exciting city in California was San Francisco. It was 140 miles from Sutter's sawmill.

Still, it was the closest port to the goldfields. It became known as the Golden Gate, and it grew faster than any other city in California. In 1848, less than a thousand people lived in San Francisco. Five years later, fifty thousand people lived there.

Its streets were muddy and crowded with people from all over the world. Many languages were spoken, including German, Chinese, French, and Spanish.

In San Francisco, there were bullfights, circuses, and theaters. However, gambling was the most popular form of entertainment. Street gamblers set up card games under tents. Gambling halls like the Bella Union were in fancy buildings. They were decorated with chandeliers and mirrors. Piles of gleaming gold sat on their tables. Some miners would play card games like faro or poker. They might lose all their hard-earned gold in one game. Where there was gambling, there was usually smoking and drinking. Sometimes there were fistfights or gunfights.

In the summer of 1849, the San Francisco harbor was full of ships. Abandoned ships. About two hundred of them. Their crews and captains had all gone prospecting. Who could blame them? Sailors only earned ten dollars a month. They'd heard prospectors could earn that much in less than a day.

By 1850, there were more than six hundred abandoned ships in the harbor. Many eventually rotted and sank. Others were taken apart, so that the wood could be used for new buildings. But dozens of ships were dragged ashore. Entire

ships got turned into warehouses or saloons. A ship named the *Niantic* became a hotel that made $20,000 a month! Another named the *Euphemia* became the city's first prison.

Henry Wells, William Fargo, and others began a stagecoach mail service in March of 1852. Their six-horse coaches were red with yellow wheels. A green treasure box was kept under the driver's feet. It carried gold nuggets, business documents, and mail. Travel from San Francisco to St. Louis, Missouri, took about three weeks. This business grew into Wells Fargo & Company. It operates a large chain of banks today.

Businessmen and miners began to bring their families out west. San Francisco slowly became more civilized. Schools and churches were built. Fancy shops opened. An Italian named Domingo Ghirardelli began selling candy in 1852. His shop grew into the Ghirardelli Chocolate Company. It has been in business for more than 160 years.

Silver

The biggest silver strike in the United States was in Nevada in 1859. No one is sure who discovered it. Some say it was two brothers named Ethan and Hosea Grosh. But the silver was named the Comstock Lode, after Henry Comstock. He claimed some of the Grosh brothers' land after they died.

An investor and a partner in a mine on the Comstock Lode, George Hearst was an expert miner and successful businessman. He grew fabulously wealthy and became a US senator. He was also the father of William Randolph Hearst, a famous newspaperman.

Men who'd gotten rich in the West had the money to bring culture and refinement to the city. They wanted it to become like New York, Paris, or London. Their money and power would help these dreams come true.

Klondike Gold Rush

Two prospectors found gold while fishing in a creek off the Klondike River in 1896. This was in northwest Canada's Yukon Territory (Alaska today). The news sparked a huge gold rush. By 1897, one hundred thousand miners had come from all over the world.

The Klondike was hard to reach. It was snowy and freezing cold. Miners had to carry supplies up steep, icy mountains. Some fell to their deaths. Less than half of them would make it to the mountains and forests where the gold had been found. If they did make it, the gold digging was hard. Frozen soil called permafrost covered much of the land. Only about four thousand miners actually found any gold. But some got rich.

In 1903, an author named Jack London wrote a book set during the Klondike gold rush: *The Call of the Wild*. People were fascinated by gold rushes. The book became very popular and is still read widely today.

CHAPTER 9
Mining Gets Harder

A few years after the strike at Sutter's sawmill, the easy gold was gone. Most miners weren't finding enough to pay for food and supplies. There were still plenty of gold deposits in California. The problem was that they were hidden. The gold was wedged deep inside mountains or underground.

Hard rock (usually quartz) with gold veins in it is called ore. Miners began tunneling for ore. They dug into rocky hillsides using shovels, picks, and drills. There was a lot of guesswork involved. Some tried to locate veins of gold by using magic. They wore necklaces with charms that were said to be gold magnets. They

also tried using forked tree branches called divining rods. They believed the branches would twitch when gold was near.

Thousands of miles of tunnels were dug and blasted with dynamite. Miners would go hundreds or even thousands of feet down a tunnel opening in a rickety elevator. Working deep inside the tunnel, they filled buckets or ore cars with rock. Then they hauled the rock outside. The ceiling of a tunnel was supported by wooden beams. Sometimes these broke or fell over. Then there would be a cave-in. Some miners got buried alive. Explosions and poisonous gases in a tunnel could kill miners, too.

To get the gold out of the ore, the rock had to be crushed. A machine with huge hammers called a stamp pounded the ore to dust. Then the gold dust was separated from the rock dust. A chemical called mercury was used in this process. Back then, miners called it quicksilver. They didn't know it was poisonous. When they heated it to separate the gold, it produced a vapor that could make them sick.

This kind of mining didn't turn out to be very profitable. Even worse, it hurt the environment. Mercury got washed into streams, where it killed fish and other wildlife.

A new, faster way of mining called hydraulic mining began. Miners aimed high-pressure water hoses at hillsides. The powerful jets of water hit the base of the hills hard. They ate away at the dirt that supported the top of the hill. Once the bottom was worn away, the top crashed down in a landslide.

Hills tumbled down into piles of gravel. Huge trees were swept away in the downward rush of dirt and rock. Meadows and valleys below were

buried. Farmland was destroyed. Farmers and other people protested. Eventually, laws were made to protect the land.

Dredge mining was another quick mining method. Machines called dredges scooped gravel from the bottoms of deep lakes and rivers. Only big companies could buy the large, costly equipment. Instead of working for themselves, many miners worked for the companies. They got paid by the day. It became impossible for them to strike it rich. Any gold they found belonged to the company.

Some forty-niners left California. They went to try their luck at silver mining in Nevada's Comstock Lode. Many gave up and headed back east. The westward rush for gold slowed down.

Boomtowns spring up when something brings people there in a hurry. Like a discovery of gold or oil. But if the gold or oil runs out, the towns can die off. Some mining camps survived. Hangtown grew into the city of Placerville. Others, like Bidwell's Bar, became ghost towns. Saloons, banks, and hotels that had been wildly busy were suddenly empty. Grass began to grow

between the slats of wooden sidewalks. Wind and rain eventually knocked over tents and buildings. After a while, it was like the town had never existed. Some ghost towns are now tourist sites.

CHAPTER 10
How the Gold Rush Changed America

With amazing speed, the gold rush sent settlers westward. When James Marshall first found gold at the lumber mill, only about 30,000 people lived in California. Twelve years later, the population had swelled to 380,000. All those people needed to eat. Farms and ranches sprang up all around California.

Gold made California important to the United States. Only about thirty months after the Mexican-American War ended, California became a state. This happened far sooner than it might have without the gold rush.

Because of the gold rush, people came to California from all over the world. They added to the culture of the United States and played an important part in great events. For instance, Chinese workers helped build the transcontinental railroad of 1869. It went from Nebraska to California. After it opened, the trip west only took one week!

Thousands of westbound gold-seekers passed through Missouri. There, some saw slave auctions for the first time. It turned many against the idea of slavery.

The gold rush was a disaster for Native Americans. In 1848, there were 150,000 Native Americans in California. Twelve years later, there were only 30,000. Some had been pushed out to make way for settlers. Others had been murdered or had died from hunger or disease. Native Americans had lived on the land first. But because of westward expansion, they lost their way of life.

The two men who'd started it all were ruined by the gold rush. James Marshall managed to get by doing odd jobs. He also would sign autographs as souvenirs. He died in a small, poor cabin. John Sutter lost much of his fortune.

There would be other gold rushes in America. They'd happen in other states such as Arizona and Montana. And in other places like Australia, South Africa, Wales, and Scotland. But the California gold rush was one-of-a-kind. It didn't just change California. It changed the United States forever. Now the country reached from the Atlantic to the

Pacific. Or as the song "America the Beautiful" says, from sea to shining sea.

The gold rush had lasted less than five years. Most prospectors who came never got rich. But they had seen amazing sights and been part of a great adventure. They would never forget the good, bad, thrilling days of the California gold rush!

Timeline of the Gold Rush

1799	The North Carolina gold rush begins
1821	California becomes Mexican territory
1829	The Georgia gold rush begins
1834	John Sutter moves from Switzerland to the United States
1839	Sutter builds a fort at the crossing of the Sacramento and American Rivers
1846	The Mexican-American War begins
1847	James Marshall begins building Sutter's lumber mill on the American River
1848	James Marshall discovers gold at Sutter's sawmill on January 24
	California becomes part of the United States when the Mexican-American War ends on February 2
	The first newspaper report of Marshall's gold strike appears on March 15
	Sam Brannan fuels gold fever in San Francisco in May

Sutter's bookkeeper, John Bidwell, strikes gold in July

President James K. Polk confirms the California gold discovery in December

1850 All non-American miners in California are taxed

California becomes America's thirty-first state on September 9

Levi Strauss comes to San Francisco

1859 Silver is discovered in Nevada's Comstock Lode

1880 John Sutter dies

1885 James Marshall dies

Timeline of the World

1845	Elias Howe invents the sewing machine
	James K. Polk is sworn in as president of the United States
	Disease strikes the potato crop in Ireland and many starve in the Irish Potato Famine
1846	The planet Neptune is discovered
1848	Lucretia Mott and Elizabeth Cady Stanton hold the first women's rights conference at Seneca Falls, New York
1849	Elizabeth Blackwell becomes the first female doctor in the United States
1851	The Great Exhibition is held in London
	A gold rush begins in Australia
1852	Harriet Beecher Stowe publishes *Uncle Tom's Cabin*
1853	Oregon's Willamette University is the first university established west of the Rockies
1854	Florence Nightingale nurses British soldiers in Asia during the Crimean War

1855 —	A railroad connecting the Atlantic and Pacific Oceans opens in Panama
1858 —	The first telegraph is sent by transatlantic cable
1859 —	Abolitionist John Brown leads a raid against the US arsenal at Harpers Ferry
—	Charles Darwin publishes *On the Origin of Species*
1860 —	The Pony Express mail service begins
1861 —	Abraham Lincoln is sworn in as president of the United States
—	The US Civil War begins
1869 —	The First Transcontinental Railroad is finished
1914 —	The Panama Canal opens

Bibliography

Blumberg, Rhoda. *The Great American Gold Rush.*
New York: Bradbury Press, 1989.

Brands, H. W. *The Age of Gold.* New York: Doubleday, 2002.

*Friedman, Mel. *The California Gold Rush.*
New York: Children's Press, 2010.

*Ito, Tom. *The California Gold Rush.* San Diego: Lucent Books, 1997.

*Kalman, Bobbie. *The Gold Rush.* New York: Crabtree Publishing Company, 1999.

Ketchum, Liza. *The Gold Rush.* Boston: Little, Brown, 1996.

*Krensky, Stephen. *Striking It Rich.* New York: Aladdin Paperbacks, 1996.

*Schanzer, Rosalyn. *Gold Fever!* Washington, DC: National Geographic Society, 1999.

*Sherrow, Victoria. *Life During the Gold Rush.* San Diego: Lucent Books, 1998.

*Walker, Paul Robert. *Gold Rush and Riches.* New York: Kingfisher, 2011.

*Books for young readers